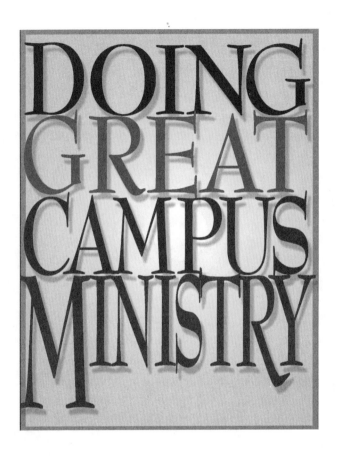

DOING GREAT CAMPUS MINISTRY

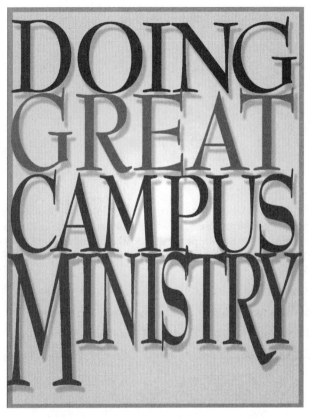

DOING GREAT CAMPUS MINISTRY

Angela Hallahan, C.H.F., Editor

ave maria press Notre Dame, Indiana

International Standard Book Number: 0-87793-996-9

Cover and text design by Katherine Robinson Coleman

Printed and bound in the United States of America.

Library of Congress Cataloging-in-Publication Data

Doing great campus ministry : a guide for Catholic high schools / Angela Hallahan, editor.

    p. cm.

Includes bibliographical references.

    ISBN 0-87793-996-9 (pbk.)

  1. Church work with students--Catholic Church. 2. Church work with students--United States. 3. Catholic high school students--United States--Religious life. I. Hallahan, Angela (Angela Mary)

BX2347.8.S8D65 2003
259'.23--dc21

                           2003007348

Contents

Introduction

THE DAILY CHALLENGES HIGH SCHOOL campus ministers face appear both overwhelming and daunting; yet they are challenges that can be met by those who accept campus ministry as the sacred trust it is. Such is the focus and viewpoint of this welcome and timely contribution to the subject.

Written *by* campus ministers *for* campus ministers, *Doing Great Campus Ministry* draws on the prayerful reflection, lived experience, and tried practice of its five authors, and will prove to be an essential, effective and practical resource. Campus ministers and campus ministry teams, who seek direction in this ministry so vital to a lived Christianity within our high schools, will find in this text a simple, clear user-friendly guide for truly doing exceptional ministry.

Doing Great Campus Ministry has been compiled by five experienced campus ministers to focus on five essential elements:

STEVE WICKSON outlines in Chapter One, "Campus Ministry: A Specialized Ministry in the 21st Century," the need for campus ministers to be well grounded in their own faith so that by God's word and his or her witness, it will be communicated not only to the students but to the entire faith community of the school.

KATHLEEN NICHOLAS has been in ministry with youth for thirty years. In the past eight years at Louisville High School she has worked to build a ministry on her campus that the students can call their own, drawing from the transforming charism of the Sisters of St. Louis who founded the school. She envisions the director of campus ministry to be the one who fans the flame of vision and mission in the school, and who keeps the charism of the school alive and evident.

Sr. Una Feeney, S.S.S., has spent many years ministering to and with youth. Currently, she is director of campus ministry at Providence High School in Burbank, California. She knows that while it does not always happen, it is necessary that the campus minister take some "time out" to look at the importance of taking "Care of the Campus Minister."

George Meade, with thirteen years of campus ministry experience, believes that all campus ministers need to know the "nuts and bolts" of the practical dimension of this ministry. In Chapter Four, "Eight to Three and Three to Eight", one will find meaningful and creative ways to get a campus ministry team up and running as well as ways to build on your current efforts.

Sr. M. Beatrice Garcia, R.S.M., is another longtime campus minister. In Chapter Five, "Continuity of the School's Vision and Mission," she challenges campus ministers to be organized. She encourages all to call on the gifts and capabilities of the school community, always remembering that the campus ministry team is the guardian of the Catholic identity of the school.

For me, personally, it is both an awesome and exciting experience to serve in campus ministry. It calls for deep faith, sustained hope, and a compassionate and generous love. It requires, moreover, that the ministers be attentive to realizing the precious gift they are beyond the school community to the Church at large, and the need to care for themselves amid the frustrations that will inevitably arise. *Doing Great Campus Ministry* has been compiled by campus ministers who have known the joys and rewards of the ministry, while at the same time acknowledging the frustrations inherent in such a program. These authors offer their experience and do indeed speak "with authority."

I believe campus ministry is the heartbeat of the school community. This manual will be a valuable tool for ministers just beginning or a fresh look for those who have served with dedication and commitment over the years. Whichever group you find yourself in, may you go forth with the words of St. Paul in your hearts:

Be awake to all dangers

Stand firm in your faith

Be brave and be strong

And may everything you
do be done with love.

—1 Corinthians 16:13–14

Sr. Angela Hallahan, C.H.F.
Director of Certification,
Religion Coordinator, Secondary Schools,
Archdiocese of Los Angeles

I

Campus Ministry: A Specialized Ministry in the 21st Century

BY STEVE WICKSON

St. Monica Catholic High School

CAMPUS MINISTRY HAS BEEN A CRUCIAL aspect of high schools (and colleges) for most of the last century, but it has only been in recent years that campus ministry has been understood as a highly specialized ministry that requires training, continuing education, support, and vision for the minister. The days when a campus minister can be named solely based on being young, energetic, enthusiastic, or a recent graduate from a Catholic college are hopefully over. Also, campus ministers have often been treated as "jack of all trades," asked to do administrative work, teach one class or more, or serve only on a part-time basis at the school.

Formation, not appointment, of campus ministers is absolutely crucial today. Ideally then, a campus minister is a full-time minister, like a pastor in a parish, who can devote exclusive time to supporting and nurturing this vital ministry presence on campus. If additional duties are required of the campus minister, we understand, but this is not the ideal situation.

Formation of Campus Ministers and Campus Ministry

The first supposition in understanding campus ministry for the twenty-first century is that it must be the lifeblood of the Catholic high school campus. These corollaries then follow:

✦ *Campus ministry is a specialized ministry to which people are called.*

✦ *Campus ministers must be formed, not named or appointed.*

✦ *Campus ministers require support, training, and ongoing spiritual development.*

In the past, when most Catholic schools were affiliated with a parish, it was often an associate pastor or curate who may have served as campus minister. He would have had seminary training, usually consisting of philosophy, four years of theology, and pastoral supervision, before being assigned to serve as campus minister. In more recent years, as men and women religious served in this role, those appointed would have had two years of novitiate training and several years of formation besides their academic training. We should desire no less formational training for laity who are now named campus ministers. A minimum training of two years, including mentoring and supervision by an experienced campus minister, is necessary for any person without theological or pastoral training.

So how do we form a campus minister? First, consider a theological context for ministry. For purposes of this article, ministry will be defined as "spiritual participation in the life and vision of Jesus, seeking to bring his love, reconciliation and hope to those in need." All baptized Catholics are called to share in the priesthood of Christ. There is a distinct apostolate of the laity, but some are called to certain kinds of leadership which require specialized training.[1] Additionally, campus ministry must be seen as the task of the entire school faith community and not solely the task of the one with the title. *Everyone on the campus must be called to share in the ministry and see his or her role as being campus minister.* The one with the title "campus minister" is better named the "Director of Campus Ministry." The director or facilitator is called to help empower others to claim their role as co-workers as part of a community of ministers, each called to participate in the ministry of Christ and each requiring appropriate training for his or her role.

If the campus minister's first role is to call forth the talent of the community, then further elements of a campus minister's job description are:

✚ *Providing Spiritual Vision*

✚ *People Management*

✚ *Enforcing Boundaries and Limits*

✚ *Empowerment*

✚ *Delegation*

Notice the skills are less about *doing* and more about *helping others* to do. A campus minister must model himself or herself after Jesus, who empowered others to heal, preach, and teach in his name. Jesus called forth special talents of his disciples. A campus minister must do as Jesus did, but must also be willing to accept the role of Jesus' first disciples who were sometimes confused, asked for help, and did not pretend to have all the answers. In fact, Jesus' disciples were often perplexed by Jesus' teaching and uncertain about what was expected of them.[2] As a disciple, one seeks to follow Jesus and demonstrate a lived awareness of how a relationship with Christ affects all aspects of a person's life. One becomes committed to living and witnessing justice and compassion, but is also mindful of one's humanness and vulnerability.

Within this context let us now add several skills required to be a successful disciple who finds herself or himself as a campus minister:

✚ *A campus minister works well with others as co-workers, with no need to be in charge.*

✚ *A campus minister empowers and supports others as colleagues.*

✝ *A campus minister is a good listener, attentive to the struggles of others in their ministry.*

✝ *A campus minister has a deep, intimate connection with Christ.*

✝ *A campus minister is able to dialogue with Christ about the everyday concerns of his or her life.*

The disciples knew that they could not do ministry alone; they needed each other. Each needed to answer the question that Jesus asked Peter and the other disciples: "Who do you say that I am?" A campus minister must be able to answer this question for each day, each event, and each school year.

Jesus preached a reign of God that is present both now and for the future. What this means is that God's power will be radically present in the events of the day and even more present in the events of the future. Campus ministry must be about this same message. The reign of God is upon us, within us, in our midst, and just as radically present on our campus and in our ministry! The power of what we do in the simple events of our campus ministry takes on new meaning because of this vision.

Whether it is writing a letter, setting up chairs, or washing dishes—all activities are now a different task because they are about building the reign of God. All events and programs in campus ministry must be connected to this vision. All students, faculty, administrators, parents, and members of the community must see their roles as part of the vision of campus ministry. It is the primary role of the campus minister to instill this kind of consciousness, so that campus ministry is not just like any other program or extracurricular activity on campus. When all campus ministers and those who assist in any way clearly see their labor as *participation* in Jesus' ministry, they realize that they too are disciples called to help build the kingdom that Jesus proclaimed.

When this connection with Jesus' ministry is the focus, community occurs quite spontaneously, because each person in the school sees his or her role as part of this common task. We are all building God's reign together; we are all participating in a common endeavor; therefore, we are all united. Without such a vision and sensitivity, campus ministry will be subject to the same forces of division and factionalism as other activities. Sexism, racism, ageism, favoritism, or whatever fills a campus with various cliques or factions will win out unless we are called to a greater vision of being a part of a true community. Campus ministry is the one activity on campus that must go beyond such separation and create a community based on one common task: We are all building the reign of God.

Creating a vibrant, inclusive community that mirrors the kingdom is not an easy task, but it is the most essential task of the campus minister. For the new director of campus ministry, there is some initial good news and bad news! Let's get the bad news out of the way first: The bad news is that the task you are about to engage in, namely building a visible example of the reign of God on your campus, is a formidable one and one that is never completed. It can always be improved upon, renegotiated, and critiqued—and it will be. Your ministry is open-ended and will call you to continuous activity, numerous nights and weekends of work, some stress, and possible burnout within three years, unless you have begun to create a community on campus that supports and nourishes you.

The good news is really *the* Good News: Jesus will be with you in all that you do. You are not alone. You not only have the promise of Jesus' presence, but also the promise of the Holy Spirit to guide you, comfort you, inspire you, and support you. If you can be humble enough to ask for help and generous enough to empower all segments of your campus, you will be surprised beyond all belief and fulfilled beyond all expectations.

The major challenge that awaits any campus minister is teaching others that *they* are members of the campus ministry team. Together, with you, they will help bring about God's reign on the campus. As you look for colleagues in this ministry, look first to the students, faculty, and administrators.

You will need a strong alliance with the principal, who hopefully sees herself or himself as the spiritual leader of the campus and your most crucial partner.

You will need collaborators in the faculty who see campus ministry as central to the campus and to creating a spirit that permeates the entire campus, yet is distinct from all other campus groups.

You will also need a core group of students who clearly identify themselves as campus ministers. These students may be part of a campus ministry class, elective, club, or some other group that already has an interest or a sense of calling to campus ministry.

Additionally, do not be afraid to seek participation from parents, the local parish youth minister, or campus ministry directors from other high schools. These people may not step forward without being asked, but they are usually more than willing to share their particular kinds of help. Merely putting an announcement in the church bulletin or school newsletter with a general call for "anyone interested in helping" is not the same as a particular invitation to a particular person to do a particular task.

When you need help, ask the people who are likely to say "yes" and ask them to do a concrete task. After they complete their task, be sure to thank them and invite them to consider being part of the ministry. Next, try to include them in an awareness of what campus ministry is. This is when you share your vision about building God's reign and participating in the ministry of Christ. Encourage your volunteers to read a scripture account about the disciples or a Church document, such as *The Decree on the Apostolate of the Laity*. You may even want to have a follow-up session about how we are all called to be ministers. By nurturing your volunteers, you are on your way to creating the team that will sustain you.

Besides working to create a team, you must constantly deepen your own spirituality and dependence on God. No matter what other practical information this book may share, always remember that your most essential help is "in the Lord" (also see Chapter 2).

You cannot pray too much or too often. In your personal prayer ask for God's help whenever it is needed. In your public prayer, be ready to let others see your intimacy with Christ. Pray from the heart with no fear about how it will be perceived. Remember, much of your ministry is by modeling, so be prepared to model a humble, prayerful disciple who is confident of his or her mission and is always in need of Christ's companionship and the support of a nurturing community.

Praxis of Campus Ministry Related to the Vision

Applying a vision of building God's reign to the lived reality of campus ministry is called the *praxis* of campus ministry. The praxis is your ministry in the school to which you minister with all its history, expectations, personalities, and other unique elements. The reality of your school may involve a very busy campus ministry with a retreat program, liturgies, Christian service, prayer rituals, and social events already in place or, oppositely, very few of these. Your first step is to evaluate the quality and quantity of your programming. There is a tendency to add to what your predecessor did. The net result is a campus ministry program that continues to grow and may have too many "sacred cows." By sacred cow I mean events, programs, or procedures that have happened in the past and are expected to be repeated *ad infinitum*. One of the first challenges is to reflect on each program and see how it fits with your overall vision for the ministry. Questions you may want to ask:

- *Are there too many programs?*
- *Are there too many events?*
- *How well does each program serve the overall ministry?*

The challenge is to reflect and evaluate the schedule each year, but be prepared for resistance from those who had invested in creating each particular program. Politically, the safest course is to keep the program the same the first year with only a few modifications and personal touches, but the program should reflect your vision and more importantly the theological context discussed earlier.

If your program needs to be developed from scratch or significantly revised, consider core elements first:

1. *Prayer*

2. *Service*

3. *Faith Development*

Use these three priorities or whatever priorities you and your principal determine are necessary for your new school. Be careful not to create a program by choosing one with too many events and with little time for reflection. It is probably best to decide on a few key areas for the year and develop a mission statement and a program that supports them.

The mission statement provides a vision for your campus ministry. It should be written in a clear and distinct paragraph of three to four sentences that detail your priorities. A few objectives can be established for each priority.

These objectives should be measurable and give you a concrete way to evaluate your program each year. For example, if the priority is faith development of the students and faculty, sample objectives could be such things as having one retreat each semester, or developing a faith-sharing group that meets weekly. Notice how the mission statement is abstract and develops a vision, which is obtained by certain objectives, which can then be measured by concrete accomplishments.

Without such reflection and planning it is easy for campus ministry to take on a momentum of its own. The year can develop as an endless series of events—one followed ever so quickly by the next, with no sense of the importance or priority. As such campus ministry can become perpetual busyness, but not necessarily the building of God's reign as defined earlier.

Remember: there are an infinite number of good things that can be accomplished in campus ministry, but you cannot do them all. One of the responsibilities of the director is to help prioritize activities. Deciding on events and the use of your time should be based on these priorities. Otherwise, the hundreds of good ideas that will emerge will result in hundreds of activities and events with no rhyme or reason to them. If you don't have control of the calendar, it will control you and eventually consume you. Like a pastor in a parish, you are the pastor of the school community who must decide a direction and develop focal points for parish outreach. Recall the advice of St Francis: do few things, but do them well. Heart-felt dreams go slowly.

Meeting the Demands of Campus Ministry

There are times when all the demands of campus ministry can be overwhelming—retreats to be planned, liturgies you want to be inspiring, and dealing pastorally with students who have personal concerns. We must never forget that Jesus himself was never too busy to respond to an individual in need. Recall the story of the hemorrhaging woman who sought to touch the garment of Jesus. At first Jesus seems irritated by being sidetracked from his mission for that day, but his stopping and tending to her must always be our model. Students with needs, whether profound or mundane, must always be the priority. They are never interruptions; they are the ministry. One way to conceive of campus ministry is as a series of "interruptions," each of which offers an opportunity to model Christ's availability and compassion.

As we look back to Jesus' model, we must always view the reign of God as *present* reality. We learn from Jesus that the person who enters our life is the focal point of all of our attention. With respect to campus ministry this means that the person who walks through the door is the most important person in the world and the focal point of all our attention and kindness for that moment. This moment and this person represent the true initiation of God's reign. We must never lose sight of our ministry in terms of responding directly and compassionately to those in need.

Jesus also teaches that the kingdom is also emergent, growing, always unfolding, and only to be fully realized in the future. The good news for us is that we need never see God's reign as exhausted, even though we ourselves may have this feeling at times. God's reign is made new and refreshed each time we have an opportunity to minister. God's reign itself keeps growing and emerging because there will always be new people to serve. The true presence of God will be made manifest by our interactions with others in the way that Jesus taught.

Jesus recognized the need to empower others to help build God's reign. He chose his disciples as a model to us of how best to operate, namely as a team, with fervent coworkers, each with a passion and mission of their own. In our example above of a ministry directly responsive to the needs of students, a wonderful opportunity exists to name others to be a part of your "ministry of presence," that welcoming, hospitable group which receives each student with focused attention. Practically, you may not be able to be present to each person, but you can facilitate others to share in this ministry. What a wonderful opportunity for some peer ministers, faculty leaders, parents, or grandparents to be available for those students who drop in while you may be teaching a class or engaged in other duties.

Creating a team and building a community become the concrete manifestations of our desire to do as Jesus did. Consider the role that Jesus played with his disciples: he called them forth, trained them by spending privileged time with them in prayer and service, and empowered them to follow his example. These dynamics become the dynamics that we seek to emulate in creating a community. Jesus was always the heart of the ministry; he had the vision and the perspective about what was to come and what could be. Likewise, it is the director of campus ministry who must supply the vision, but must constantly welcome others, invite others, and empower others.

A group of twenty to twenty-five carefully selected students will be an invaluable asset to any campus ministry program and represent the equivalent of Jesus' core disciples. Such students could be selected after a comprehensive interview process that should include some input from the faculty, the administration, and student leaders. Once a team is selected, they should be brought together for a retreat before the school year begins. This orientation retreat will have three goals:

1. *To help students to bond, connect, and get to know each other.*

2. *To help students develop a sense of themselves as ministers.*

3. *To develop a mission statement with clear objectives for the year.*

As discussed earlier, a mission statement should be drafted only after an informed discussion has occurred between the principal, the student leadership team, and the campus minister to determine the priorities for the year. These priorities may be discussed with the student leaders during an initial retreat or first meeting. The idea is to be clear that the priorities chosen are somewhat non-negotiable and that they are be the foundation for the entire program and mission statement.

A new mission statement, based on these priorities, may be drafted by the team during the orientation retreat or very early in the first semester. Besides drafting a mission statement, the primary role of the student team is to determine one to three objectives within each priority that will be their goals for the coming year. Strategy about how to move toward accomplishing these concrete objectives might include committees, a complete team effort, or shifting priorities throughout the year. It is the responsibility of the campus minister to name clear priorities; the team's responsibility is to create a mission statement and measurable objectives, which it will seek to do during the year.

Your role as campus minister is to make sure the ministry happens, not to try to do everything by yourself. The single greatest threat to a successful ministry is the so-called "messiah complex," a spoken or unarticulated feeling that we can and must do the entire job by ourselves. The surest guarantee of frustration and likely burnout is the feeling that we are alone in doing the ministry.

Respecting our own limits and the limits of hours in a day gently calls us back to humility and reality. We can never do all that needs doing in campus ministry by ourselves; a team of coworkers is essential. Our role is to empower others to join us and never pretend that we alone can do all that is needed. Recall the simple maxim that we are called to be master builders, not magicians.

No matter how well one understands and accepts this wisdom, there will be times for every campus minister when she or he feels exhausted, overextended, or frustrated. Such moments can also be moments of grace if we use them to reflect back on our ministry and prayerfully review what has transpired. For example, if after some event you feel tired, angry, frustrated, burdened, or unappreciated you may want to review the event with these questions:

✠ *Am I doing too much by myself?*

✠ *Which tasks could have been delegated?*

- ✠ *Did I give those with responsibility enough trust and support to accomplish their task?*

- ✠ *Who else could have been asked to participate?*

- ✠ *Which tasks should someone other than me have done?*

Remember, your most important role is to envision and empower, not to micromanage. For example, imagine your campus ministry is responsible for hosting a reception for new students, but on reflection you find you did most of the work and organization. Stop! Review the event with the loving eyes of Christ. Ask for the grace to see the moments when others offered to help, or when some others looked like they wanted to be involved. This moment of frustration can be a moment of grace if you can learn how it could be done differently for the future.

Skills of delegation are often best learned by one of two events where you clearly overextended and did too much. Every campus minister overextends at times in their ministry, but those who will survive must learn from such experiences and gently call themselves back to the skills of delegation. Remember, delegation requires asking a particular person for particular help for a particular task. Few people will say "no" if asked personally and directly to assist in a reasonable way. In fact they may be waiting to be asked. Letting them help is allowing them to share in the ministry. Empowerment happens when we ask for help and then step out of the way. Let us review the sequence of creating a team ministry related to a specific event:

1. *Ask for help.*

2. *Clarify the task.*

3. *Get out of the way.*

4. *Support the team as needed.*

5. *Thank each person sincerely, publicly, and in a timely fashion.*

Necessary Boundaries of Campus Ministry

••

We have seen the necessity for campus ministers to create boundaries with their time. We would not do justice to any discussion of campus ministry unless we spoke about a series of boundaries, both personal and professional, that are crucial for campus ministers. By boundaries, I mean behaviors that seek to protect the integrity of our ministry, ourselves, and those we serve.[3] A campus minister must be aware of five types of boundaries:

1. *professional boundaries*

2. *personal boundaries*

3. *time boundaries*

4. *relationship boundaries*

5. *issues of confidentiality*

A campus minister is a professional and is held to the same level of expected behavior as any other professional: polite, courteous, responsible behavior that allows one to deliver a service without any other agenda. Yet a campus minister is held to even higher standards. Because of the trust that is associated with their role and because of the need to create an environment of unambiguous love and trust, a campus minister must have clear and distinct personal boundaries, which reflect the relationship of trust and the fact that we model Jesus' love to those we serve. As such, our relationships must always be based on the growth and safety of the other and not our own needs.

It is *never* appropriate to develop any type of romantic interest or intimacy with those we serve or even friendships as if the students were our peers. Time boundaries and personal boundaries keep our ministry separate from our personal life and protect us and those we serve. These boundaries are designed to help us maintain a personal life distinct from our ministry and to guarantee that all can come freely seeking the visible sign of Jesus' love and acceptance that we offer. In order to do this we need time away from our ministry, including regular days off, reasonable limits to our work hours, and a supportive pattern of intimacy apart from our ministry.

Because of the intensity of what we do and the deep overlapping of shared vision with our student team, it is easy to confuse this common commitment with friendship or real intimacy. We must be clear that these needs must come from other sources in our life than our ministry in order to maintain definite boundaries. There is always a temptation to blur these relationship boundaries and feel a sense of caring or friendship with those we serve, but such a posture, even with the purest of intentions, is very dangerous and highly suspect.

It is easy for others to misread our intentions or mistake our caring as an invitation to a level of intimacy that we do not intend. Jealousy or rivalries may also develop between members of the team with each seeking your affirmation or approval. Such dynamics can destroy a team and undermine the ministry. Therefore, for reasons of protecting the quality and reputation of your ministry, the sanctity of your own personal life, and the need for others to have their own relationships and intimacy outside of the ministry, the safest posture is to never conflate ministry and personal relationships. Just as one would not want to have dinner with his or her therapist, likewise one should not have a personal relationship with students and those we serve. The best boundaries are clear and distinct and ensure all students access to your caring and visible sign of God's love with no ambiguity, no hidden agenda, and no possible misunderstanding.

Another boundary for campus ministers includes issues of confidentiality. In the course of our work we may serve as pastoral counselors to our students and faculty. The confidentiality of this relationship is sacrosanct. Like other therapists, it can only be violated in situations of possible suicide or serious risk of harm to some other person. Students and faculty must be constantly made aware of our need to report such issues if they arise. As educators, campus ministers are also mandated reporters and must report instances of physical or sexual abuse, either current or in the past to your local child protection service agency.[4]

Beyond all the legal requirements, there is an immense moral responsibility that one carries by seeking to participate in the ministry of Jesus and by being a representative of Jesus' love and compassion. We only need reflect on the recent history of abuse within the Church to be reminded how profound and tragic the consequences of boundary violations are. The Church suffers, the minister suffers and those whose boundaries are violated suffer a lifetime of shame, betrayal, and anger when boundaries are not respected. Hopefully the Church of the future will be more vigilant in responding to the egregious boundary violations, but our task is to learn from this tragic episode the necessity of clear and distinct boundaries from the beginning.

We began this article with a sense of how unique and specialized campus ministry is. We must end with an even greater appreciation for its value and necessity for our campuses. When we create the team that makes it happen, and when we develop a community of love and trust where others will feel safe, we become representatives of the presence of a loving God in our world. It is an awesome task and one which we can never do alone. Let us be humble enough to ask for God's assistance by our posture of constant prayer, wise enough to realize we must create and empower a team of others to work with us, and courageous enough to maintain our boundaries so that we may experience the in-breaking of the reign of God on earth that campus ministry has the potential to foster.

For Reflection

✖ How do you feel called to campus ministry?

✖ Name three ways you can participate in ongoing formation for your role as campus minister.

✖ What do you view as essential tasks for developing a community of faith on campus?

✖ Name three core elements that you envision as part of your campus ministry.

✖ How do you recognize when you have been stretched beyond your limits as a campus minister?

Notes

1. Decree on the Apostolate of the Lay People.
2. See Luke 8:9, 8:25, 12:41.
3. See "Respecting the Boundaries" from the Archdiocese of Los Angeles in the Appendix.
4. See "Reporting Laws as a Mandated Reporter" in the Appendix.

2

The
Deeper
Call of
Campus
Ministry

BY KATHLEEN NICHOLAS

Louisville High School

I MAGINE YOU WERE HANDED A CANDLE AND told that it was your task to make sure that the flame never went out, no matter how the wind blew. As flames go, yours is rather bright; but like any flame it is a vulnerable light. As a campus minister, you are the keeper of this flame as you work to make present God's reign on the Catholic high school campus.

What better miniature model for the reign of God than a Catholic high school campus, a veritable field upon which the treasure of the kingdom is buried? When one considers the dreams of those who founded our high schools and the magnificent visions upon which thousands of schools have been built, one can only marvel at the wealth of inspiration that is at our fingertips. In the Catholic tradition, most of our schools were conceived out of the educational and spiritual missions of religious orders of women and men, or, in the case of parish and diocesan schools, the weaving of many charisms which held the common thread of gospel values.

When we reflect on the legacy of the great founders of religious communities, such as Francis de Sales, Clare of Assisi, Ignatius of Loyola, Louis Bautain, and Mother Seton, we see that the ultimate reality of these original visions will be carried forth and fulfilled by some who may not be members of their orders. In order to promote their legacies, a clear understanding of the nature and role of the spiritual life on campus must be examined.

The Spiritual Life

The "spiritual life" has many definitions today. In the new age realm, "being spiritual" may have nothing to do with God, but rather a way of being that is at one with the universe. Also, countless self-help books have been written about subjects like "finding oneself" and "discovering well-being." Few of these are found in the religion section of the neighborhood bookstore.

In recent generations, the effort to amass countless possessions and to be completely self-sufficient has lead to a segment of the world that lives as if it does not need God. Many eventually come to a stalemate when and where the possessions cease to bring about the expected happiness. And so, the search for spirituality begins. In this understanding, spirituality is equated with peace of mind, a way of being at one with self, others, and the world. This is very good. Many people today follow the well-worn paths of eastern religions and the spirituality of Native Americans. The folly is not that these ways of "being spiritual" are not good for the soul. The folly is the belief that there is something brand new at work here. *The heart of spirituality is simply a way of being with God.* It is the fine art of paying attention to God's presence in our lives.

One of the most poignant lessons in spirituality was taught by Moses in the book of Exodus, when he asked to see God's face. At first God said, "No." No one could see the face of God and live. But then God relented and, perhaps this is the moment that the spiritual life was conceived, because God made it possible for Moses to *be* with him.

Throughout scripture, there are numerous other lessons in the spiritual life. Elijah heard a tiny whisper, shepherds watched in the fields, Mary treasured many things in her heart, and Christ set himself apart in order to be with his Father. Mystic Julian of Norwich assures us in her writings that Christ wants us to live in constant expectation of him. So how do we as campus ministers and keepers of Christ's flame avert the attention of our students from the false promises of the world and toward expecting Christ? How do we teach their souls to listen? How do we teach their hearts to see? *We meet them where they are and draw from the spiritual gifts they already possess: their natural hunger for God and thirst for justice.* We take these gifts and weave with them the threads of the school charism—the original spirituality and educational mission of the school. This basic fabric of spirituality should be the foundation for your school's mission statement.

In order to gain insight into the nature of spirituality and the ways that spirituality grows and develops in adolescence, it is propitious to refer to the work of theologian James Fowler, who sees faith as a verb rather than a noun, since faith involves the *action* of relating to something or someone in a way that one must rely on feelings. It also involves the action of our human abilities to care and to hope. Fowler recognized six levels or stages in the development of the authentic spiritual life.

The first stage is defined as *Intuitive-Projective*. During this stage, the child bases her beliefs on those around her whom she trusts.

Stage two is the *Mythic-Literal* stage. It allows the child to recognize that there is a world outside of his experience. He can now tell the difference between reality and a fairy tale, and can sequester himself into his world of thoughts and insights. The authorities in his life include a wider range of adults beyond his parents including teachers and other role models.

The third stage is called *Synthetic-Coventional*. For the most part the teens we meet in high school have achieved this stage of spiritual development, since it coincides with the emergence of adolescence. In this stage, the child will begin to question existing authority and think for herself. More than ever, mentors in this spiritual life are necessary to guide the young person through this critical time in her life. The role of the campus minister is most needed at this time, and for most teens, very appreciated.

In stage four, *Individuative-Reflective*, the young person begins to practice a faith that he can call his own, and one he can express through his actions and decisions. Finding meaning in his life coincides with this expression of a personally crafted faith.

Stage five, which occurs for the most part beyond the developmental ages of high school students, is defined as *Conjunctive Faith*. During this stage, there is a strengthening of the efforts achieved during stage four with a more serious commitment.

The final stage, stage six, is defined as *Universalizing Faith*, and is a highly developed, mature faith, to which one can dedicate one's life. It is a faith from which all other aspects of life will naturally flow.

Understanding the levels of development of the spiritual or faith life is a prerequisite for the campus minister, if he or she is to be able to encourage his or her students toward a sense of spiritual well-being. This can only happen if the campus minister is dedicated to the spiritual life as well.

The work of a campus minister as the "keeper of the flame" is no less than the work of Christ. There is no better path to follow than his, and there are no better mentors from whom to seek advisement than those disciples who walked with him or encountered him along the way.

Meeting Teens Where They Are

in the center

of the universe

is a heart

not unlike

the one you carry.

all the love that ever is

is there

in the shape and form

of bright.

you will recognize

your own heart

in that light.

One of the most oft repeated comments heard in a high school religion classroom reflects a distinction between being spiritual and being religious. While many students have difficulty associating their beliefs with what they regard as institutional religion, they can and do believe themselves to be spiritual.

Unfortunately, to many young Catholics, the Church is often associated with a vat of controversial issues. Students define the

Church in the shadow of issues, rather than the life and Paschal mystery of Christ. The presence and power of God's grace must be recognized and named for the students.

In order to help teenagers embrace the Church they will inherit, we must meet them where they are. And where is that? Teens are praying at the beach and in the face of sunsets, rather than in their parish churches. They are volunteering in soup kitchens while missing Mass on Sundays. Meanwhile other teenagers are involving themselves in risky activities in which they are morally challenged by the lure of the materialistic world. Some are also turning to drugs, alcohol, and sexual encounters to assuage the hunger and loneliness they encounter in their lives. This is where we find them, caught in a spider web of conflicting ideals and values, reaching out in a desire to find and know themselves.

Two elements of faith that teenagers continue to respect and hold on to are their spiritual lives and their compassion for the poor and marginalized. The works of justice that are practiced by so many young people today encourage their desire to serve the needy. At the same time, their hunger for God and the unfolding graces offered in the life of the

Church, Christ's Body, must be continually cultivated.

Spiritual Development of the Campus Minister

Campus ministers must always make their own spiritual development a priority. This requires ongoing study and a well-practiced prayer life. Procuring a personal guide or spiritual director is not only suggested, but is necessary. The medieval sage, St. Aelred, wrote on the value of support from "soul friends" or spiritual companions on the journey. Soul friends are sources of encouragement and inspiration to those who have committed themselves to ministry. He wrote:

> Here we are, you and I, and I hope a third, Christ in our midst. There is no one to disturb us; there is no one to break in on our friendly chat, no one's prattle or noise of any kind will creep into this friendly solitude. Let us accept gracefully the boon of this place, time, and leisure.

Spiritual directors can be a source of strength as well as a sounding board for a campus minister. There will always be more to do in developing your own spirituality, and time will seem limited as long as there are students who need your attention and retreats and celebrations to plan and prepare for. The presence of a spiritual director can provide solace as well as some objective and practical advice, not only to a fledgling campus minister but to a seasoned one as well.

Inquire among colleagues, local religious communities, Catholic university faculties, and diocesan support staff for names of potential spiritual directors who can help you develop your own spiritual life, while at the same time you enhance the spiritual life of the campus you serve.

The Spiritual Life on Campus

A campus ministry team under the direction of the campus minister is charged with the care of the soul of the school. The liturgical calendar provides the campus minister with the perfect schedule to carry the school community through the academic year. Following Christ's life while celebrating special feasts will provide you with many resources with which to pray together as a community.

Teenagers today have grown up in homes where, for the most part, traditional Catholic language and rituals have not been taught. Many pre-Vatican II traditions are completely unfamiliar to today's generation. Campus ministry can provide a forum to not only educate teens about traditional expressions of Catholicism, but to put them into practice. For example, using incense to mark sacred space before liturgy can help to bring the attention of a large group of students to a peaceful place to begin a celebration, and can teach them the meaning of Church sacramentals in general. The visual and fragrant incense floating up into the air can also expose teens to a traditional approach to prayer, which is mystical and sacred.

Through the use of a school public address system, the campus minister can name for students particular Church feast days and refer to the daily and official prayer of the Church. Praying together with the entire school over the P.A. system can set the tone for each day and help to connect the spiritual fabric of the entire academic year. Special seasons like Advent and Lent can be acknowledged through prayer services, usually held at break time or during the lunch period.

One example of an Advent prayer service is a voluntary bi-weekly gathering called "Come to the Stable." At each celebration, a lone figure could be added to the stable scene accompanied by short prayers and petitions to help prepare students for Christmas. The infant Christ figure can be withheld from the stable scene until the students return to school, which in most cases is after the feast of the Epiphany. This will help to celebrate Christmas in its rightful season, not in the one that corresponds only to shopping days before December 25. "Come to the Stable" can be held in a school chapel or any designated spot where a stable can be recreated. If this or a similar service is planned and officiated over by the students themselves, you will find the interest and attendance will grow.

Liturgical celebrations such as the Eucharist, reconciliation services, and other prayer services are vital to the spiritual life of a high school campus. The more you involve students in the planning and preparation of these experiences, the more the entire student body will be encouraged to participate. These celebrations should follow the liturgical calendar, drawing themes from feast days and daily readings. The academic pressures of the school year can easily steer a community away from its need to live a spiritual life. It is the responsibility of the campus minister to keep that proverbial candle burning by uplifting the catholicity of the school through prayer and celebration.

Spiritual Vision:
Drawing from the Charism
of the Founders

We began this reflection describing a campus minister as a keeper of a flame—the flame of Christ—with the responsibility of never letting it go out. Campus ministry is both a source of light and a ministry of goodness on any Catholic high school campus. One of the particular responsibilities of a campus minister is to uphold the spiritual vision that created the school: the vision of the founders. If the original vision were to diminish, how would we distinguish one Catholic school from another? More importantly, how would we distinguish a Catholic school from a secular one?

Catholic education is a harbinger of hope for society and culture. Catholic education offers a value-based education to an often valueless society. In the history of the Church in the United States, religious communities of women and men founded schools to meet that need. These schools provided Catholic education with the additional caveat of matching the particular traditions and spiritualities of these communities. The Carmelites, for instance, have a Marian spirituality. The Jesuits have a holistic, forward-thinking approach. The Sisters of St. Louis work toward a world healed, unified, and transformed. The Franciscans teach simplicity. The Sisters of Social Service emphasize care for the community. Each community and its schools are more than a seat of learning. They are a candle shedding its fragile beams to a darkening world.

As a campus minister, make it part of your primary work to uncover the spirit and charism of your school (see also Chapter 5). Learn the mottoes and mission statements that tell the collective story. Weave these words and traditions into the school days. Make certain that each student who graduates from your school is marked with the emblem of the school, not only on the diploma but on his or her heart. There may no longer be active religious at your school, but their spirit that built the school should remain present. Find it, celebrate it, and share it with the entire school community.

For Reflection

....

✚ *How do you see yourself as "keeper of the flame" of Christ on your campus?*

✚ *Describe several ways you find yourself in the presence of God.*

✚ *Who is someone you imagine would make a good spiritual director for you?*

✚ *What does it mean to you to meet your teens where they are at relative to their spirituality?*

✚ *Name three practical ways for cultivating the "soul" of your school.*

3

Care
of
the
Campus
Minister

By Sr. Una Feeney, S.S.S.

Providence High School

CAMPUS MINISTRY INVOLVES SERVICE TO youth in a particular school setting. In the Catholic Christian perspective this service is done in the name of our loving God. So often we separate the call to service of others from our own spirituality and prayer lives. We set in our minds that prayer is for some "other" people who are more holy than we are. We view those professional pray-ers as ones who are contemplative and not engaged in active service or ministry to others. We may think of them as free to pray while we are mired in the trenches of youth culture with all of its commotion and clutter. This of course is not an accurate portrayal. *Campus ministry must be an expression of our own relationship with God.*

In campus ministry we are often called upon to listen with the ear of our heart to a student

who is ill, confused, lonely, or has no
direction. When we listen to a young person
with our whole being, we open ourselves to
their story and experience as part of God's
constant offer of salvation to all. In order to
partake fully in God's plan for these teens, we
too must be living in God's reality, spirit, and
presence. We see, listen, touch, and hold all
that is the reality of God's revelation of
himself to us consistently and daily.

When we come to a place in our daily lives
that sees the reflection of God in all that we
encounter, then we are truly people of prayer.
Prayer can be described simply as "listening
to the Spirit speak to our hearts." The call of
Christ to commit ourselves to God and God
alone is a challenge as is the call to be a person
of prayer. We are challenged to give our very
selves to God. It is this unconditional and
mutual love for and with God that brings us
to the service and ministry to teens on our
high school campuses. The spiritual life of the
campus minister must be nurtured and fed
with the life of God.

In order to care for ourselves in this way, we
must "go away" in both time and space for a
while and enter into an intentional time of
prayer. God calls us to be re-created in God's
own likeness at all times—every day of our
lives. But this kind of spiritual growth is on

God's time, not necessarily in correlation with the school's calendar. God seems to prefer moving gradually, not with instant messaging, but in the mode of snail mail. God's pace is a slowly emerging process that unfolds his presence. To experience the oneness of our God we must position ourselves in a place and space that is open to this process. When we take the time to develop greater intimacy with God we are able to develop greater intimacy with the youth whom we are called to serve.

What does it mean to say that campus ministers are called to "go away for a while?" Imagine being away from the phone, from the demands of the bell schedule, from the noise in the halls, and entering into complete solitude. What would it sound like? This quiet solitude allows us to hear the voice of God and leads us into deeper relationship with him.

When we go away for a day of personal recollection or take the time for a retreat, we gift ourselves with the opportunity to become more of who God wants us to be. Taking time to be one with nature, alone with one's thoughts and memories, alone with reflections on the teens you care for and minister to, and focused on God's Word is a necessary respite from a campus minister's day. Time away for prayer facilitates the spiritual dimension of our lives and fosters and deepens our potential to encounter and engage with the everyday student who crosses our path. Our response to students and fellow faculty and staff can be the response of Jesus given through us. When all is said and done, what often holds in the memory of teenagers long after they have forgotten what we have said with our words, is simply our very presence to them.

Care of Our Body

Campus ministers typically expend more time and energy planning the sophomore retreat or the latest food drive than we do planning our own personal schedules. There never seems to be enough time to pray, exercise, spend time with friends, or get away for rest and relaxation. With the hectic pace of our school calendars, it is often our bodies that feel the brunt of our busy schedules. It is faster and much more convenient to swig down a fruit smoothie and gulp a coffee espresso while driving to school than it is to sit down to a healthy breakfast. Lunch may be only a candy bar from the vending machine. We may take our dinner from a fast food drive-through in order to make it back for an evening event we have scheduled at school.

Campus ministers must be attentive to the health of our bodies, our need for rest and exercise, and proper nutrition in order to keep up with the demands of the ministry. One of the easiest ways to become aware of our diets and nutrition is to set a regular time to sit down daily for each meal. Don't skip meals. Eat healthy foods, including proper servings of fruits and vegetables. Whole foods—that is, those that are not processed—contain a higher nutrient density than processed foods. When we eat with our physical health in mind we are caring for ourselves in a holistic manner and we are reverencing the bodies that God has created in love. Food can touch practically every aspect of our lives and can affect how we feel both emotionally and physically.

Exercise is another central element of a healthy lifestyle. Exercise prevents various diseases, eases depression, aids sleep, increases muscle tone, strengthens bones, and increases the blood flow from the lungs to the heart and brain. Campus ministers do not have a regular 9-to-5 type of work schedule that easily permits an exercise routine. Nevertheless, the more consistent we can become with our exercise the healthier we become, both in mind and spirit.

There are other ways we can recreate our bodies. Going to a movie, taking a long walk, spending time with a friend, going to a museum, and laughing and being silly are among the ways we can refresh ourselves.

Our bodies are marvelous mechanisms that inform us when things are not in sync. Do you pay attention to signals from your body and your environment? You may notice a craving for sweets when your body is lacking in glucose. You may experience times when you cannot concentrate or stay focused. Maybe your body is telling you that it needs sleep. These types of feelings are ways in which our bodies tell us that we must be attentive to these physical needs. Stresses that are a part of the job of a campus minister can easily take a toll on our bodies and can lead to depression and dysfunction. We can become self-absorbed and not attentive to the teens we are called to minister to and with.

Like us, Jesus sought out rest when he was tired and food when he was hungry. Like him we have a very human need to be fed and nourished, to experience rest and renewal, and to be healthy. It is up to each one of us to care for our bodies so that we can be at our full strengths in our ministry.

Care of Our Creativity

The word create comes from the Latin for "to grow or bring forth." The concept of creativity is oftentimes a burden but more positively an invitation to growth. As campus ministers we are expected to "create" liturgies that are insightful, prayerful, and poignant while using the vehicles of contemporary music. Our task in these liturgies is to engage the teenagers to explode with the Spirit and at the same time be respectful of our worshipping tradition and the school setting. The creative process requires a balance of risk-taking and restraint. As with many parts of our ministry, this creative process is filled with a tension of opposites.

When we open ourselves to our own creativity we are opening ourselves to the creative grace of God. Creativity means using the ability to see things in new and challenging ways. It is the security of our knowing the Sacred and at the same time risking new ways in which to express our relationship with God. Being creative offers us opportunities to be spontaneous and to feel zest, passion, and a sense of adventure. We are motivated to jump into the action, affirm our inner knowing, and explore ways in which to express this relationship of the Sacred in our lives. In doing so we may discover the habitual and rote ways in which we have been living which keep us comfortable and routine while we miss the coming of the Spirit into our lives.

As campus ministers, we must be aware of our own relationship with God. When we go on day after day with the same old-same old, we are not living in such a way as to be open and present to the kids we serve. When the Spirit is held within and not given out as a means in which to grow and explode into a new life, we do a disservice to our teenagers.

Think of the many inventions that started out as projects that someone was only tinkering with. I would guess that many of these final inventions are the results of mistakes that were thrown into the junk pile. How many musicians never popped a guitar string or scratched the bow of their violin (resulting in the sound of cats screeching) when first learning to play their instruments? Some of us are fearful that we will be judged harshly by others. We may even be cautious out of the fear that others will view us as silly and foolish. We try to imagine what the parents of our students would say if they saw us acting silly.

And yet, it appears that creativity is directly related to silliness. We need to let go of the comfortable and the routine in order to explore the things that we are not aware of, the things that are unknown, the things that we do not yet know. When we are willing to risk this, we become free of our safety zone, open, and ready to seek and accept new possibilities. We become aware of new ways of looking at our ministry. In doing so, we have the chance to develop new approaches that go beyond the bounds of what is usual.

Some of us are afraid to explore our own creativity and become discouraged because we compare ourselves to the great masters of the arts. We may have always wanted to be like Mick Jagger, never mind Mozart. What we must keep in mind is that all of us have a starting point. We must begin as a seed that is planted. We must be nourished and fed so that we might begin to grow.

Being creative and experiencing our creativity takes practice and patience. The piano player must practice over and over again if he wants the sounds to express the music of his soul. The gardener will add to the pile of compost, raking it and turning it, adding more and more refuse and mulch so that eventually the pile becomes fertile and potent with new life that will benefit her garden. One of the most satisfying ways to get in touch with our creative energy is to explore the world of books. Besides the value of reading to learn more about teens and our ministry, we can read other materials for personal renewal and growth.

For example, an afternoon reading about the journey of Lewis and Clark or a book exploring the inlets of Cape Cod can open for ourselves ways in which we too are explorers. When we read that Lewis and Clark came to crossroads and split rivers, we might reflect on the rivers in our lives and the directions we might take in our ministry. Who are the harbors that offer us calm and peace when we feel the storms of conflict with students or administrators? By taking time to read and reflect on the words written by others, we can open ourselves to flowing in our own imagination and tuning into the deeper reality of our own lives.

Also, what better words to reflect on than the Word of God? After reading scripture we can get those creative juices flowing by journaling our reflections on what we read and pray over. This is a way in which we can creatively record the story of our own faith and our relationship with the Sacred. There is great value in journal keeping. We can look back and see where we have been and learn from it. We can also dream of who we are to become as we experience the journey of our lives. In journals we may find keys that have helped us in our own growth that can be applied to the teens that we listen to in our offices. We have the chance to read and reflect on the wisdom of others and how it applies in our lives. Then, we might discover ways in which to put this wisdom in a language and style that is easily related to the teens on our campuses.

Another way in which to touch on our creativity is to discover the artisan that dwells within us. The list of ways to experience our creativity is nearly unlimited. For example, to help renew your creative spirit you can:

✦ *run with your face against the wind,*

✦ *pick wildflowers from alongside a country road,*

✦ *fly a kite along the seashore,*

✦ *bake cookies with leftover Christmas candy,*

✠ *invite friends over to watch a movie marathon of your favorites.*

There are also many art media to explore, including clay, paints, collages, tissue paper, song, poetry, music, dance, and movement. When we reflect back on our childhood, can we remember the experience of finger painting? clay sculpturing? gluing log cabins from wooden sticks? Getting in touch with our creativity challenges us to take a risk to remember and even recreate those experiences.

You may want to jump right in: spread out lots of newspaper, grab a huge piece of poster paper, and feel the joy of spilling poster paint into a blob in the center of the paper. Next, plop both hands into the cool, oozy, slimy, poster paint. Let your hands move and dance across the paper. Feel them glide and slop, swoosh and splat. Let the colors emerge and let yourself go. If it sounds silly, it is! The joy and simple pleasure of finger painting frees us to remember our days as a child. It invites us to remember and look for ways to apply those memories of childhood to today as a campus minister. Being open to experiences of creativity also opens us to explore the way God continues to express himself in creation.

Being playful and silly is a way to give ourselves the gift of a renewed spirit. The joy we feel when laughter brings tears to our eyes and aches to our bellies can be very bonding. In the development of campus ministry teams, it is helpful to have laughter and silliness as part of the team building experience. It's very important that campus ministers can be silly and playful in front of their campus ministry student teams. Just remember: timing is everything. There is an appropriate time and place for such fun, always keeping in mind the proper adult-student relationship. We gift each other with our joy and positive spirit. When we do this, we give ourselves a jump start and are fueled with creative energy.

In every form of creative expression—whether drawing, writing poems, dabbing pastel colors across a canvas—we are expressing our own creative interpretation of our own world and the Sacred that moves within. We are given opportunity to share with our students our own gifts and we can invite them to explore and create their own.

For Reflection

....

✛ *How is your role as campus minister an expression of your own relationship with God?*

✛ *List several possibilities you have for getting away in time and space for personal prayer.*

✛ *Name some ways you recreate and refresh your mind and spirit to better help you function as a campus minister.*

✛ *How do you reflect the joy of life in God to your students?*

4

Campus Ministry:

Eight to Three
and
Three to Eight

BY GEORGE MEADE

St. Bonaventure High School

PRIMETIME. SOAP OPERA. FILM AT ELEVEN. Fall season. Reruns. Season premiere. Sitcom. Television and its lingo, television and its allure, television and its power have become a permanent part of our lives. We are surrounded by television programming. It can inspire us, disgust us, hypnotize us, entertain us, educate us, and dupe us. Whatever it does, we cannot escape it, and, to varying degrees, we all rely on it. Certainly, one would be hard pressed to find many people in the United States who were not watching the news on September 11, 2001.

Of course, television programming is no accident. Programmers look for the best time to reach their target audience. They are well aware of the show that precedes and the show that follows another, and they make every attempt to choose wisely to optimize the number of viewers (i.e., consumers.) They look for other ways to market the show and anything about the show that is marketable.

The goals of television seem to be clear, with making money the primary one. Fame, recognition, and entertainment are other key goals. Certainly procuring advertising is important. And the ever-present push for ratings also fuels the choices of television programmers and executives.

It also seems clear that some television stations do have loftier aspirations. The programming on public stations is generally more educational and of higher quality than that on major networks. The fact is, different stations offer different programming. For example, the offerings on cable channels are different than those offered on the "major" networks.

In the world of campus ministry, we also program. We also must look at our target audience, determine "primetimes," and make decisions about what precedes and follows an event. And, as different television stations choose different programming, different schools need different programming in the area of campus ministry. For campus ministers, there are many factors to consider, many limitations to ponder, and many personalities to deal with. There are also many joys to experience, many lives to touch, many hearts to heal, many needs to serve, and many souls to lift. Because we do all with God as our guide, with Jesus at our side, with the Holy Spirit as our breath, we know that we have a common goal.

The School Day

It was 1 p.m. on the first Friday of the month and our regular faculty meeting was about to start. I saw our social studies chairperson take out her watch, as usual, to time the athletic director's monthly presentation. That little joke between them never got old. When he did stand to speak this time, the athletic director said, "We talk a lot about what happens between 8 and 3, but I want to talk to you about what's happening between 3 and 8." He went on to remind us that although there is good education going on during the regular school day, there is just as much going on after school. He mentioned athletic and cheer practices, drama rehearsals, tutoring sessions, academic competition practices, and so on. For some reason, that phrase, "8 to 3 and 3 to 8" always stuck with me. It reinforces the notion that all hours on school grounds are a part of the school day, even lunchtime and break. And at least some of the hours from 3 to 8 are also spent in school-related activities.

So what are students doing during those hours from 3 p.m. to 8 p.m., Monday through Friday? Many are engaged in school activities. Some are working. Others are spending time in outside pursuits of volunteerism or personal enrichment, hanging out with friends, picking up their younger siblings from school, or skateboarding. Most all are spending some time doing their homework. Whatever they are doing, their lives are arranged around the school day schedule. Given that academics, sports, and co-curricular groups extend beyond 3 p.m., we must ask: What about campus ministry? How do we keep campus ministry as a part of those hours?

All of these activities can be included under the larger heading of the *school program*. One dictionary definition of the word program is "a schedule or system under which action may be taken toward a desired goal." While this chapter focuses most on the nuts and bolts of the campus ministry program, perhaps we should pause here for a moment to briefly recall the goal of campus ministry.

The goal of campus ministry should reflect the charism, mission, and philosophy of the school. One of the first tasks of a campus minister is to familiarize herself or himself with those areas which are specific to each school. I would like to offer some other images that could be goals for all campus ministry programs, regardless of their specific charism or philosophy:

✠ *Consider Noah and the ark. Noah was called by God to save what would otherwise be lost, to keep life itself going. Campus ministry is called to keep the life of Christ's message going.*

✠ *Consider Moses and the Israelites. Moses was called by God to lead the Chosen People to the Promised Land. That is a noble goal for campus ministry.*

✠ *Consider the prophets, who spoke in God's name, who pointed to injustice and exhorted the people to return to following God. Campus ministry is called to prophesy, to reconcile, and to preach.*

✝ *Consider St. Paul, who wrote, "I run toward the prize to which God calls me—life on high in Christ Jesus." Campus ministry can help all students run together toward heaven.*

Whatever your school's charism or philosophy, always remember your mission and goal. And remember that we should be more concerned about the quality of the time that is spent in campus ministry than about the number of hours. It is easy to fall into the trap of being "event-driven" or of programming because "it's the way we've always done it" or "it looks good on paper." I know, because I have fallen into that trap. Instead, we should continue to fix our eyes on Christ, to be aware of the loftier goal, to remind ourselves of our calling from God. If we can remember the reason we minister, our students will experience campus ministry from 8 to 3 and recall it when they need it from 3 to 8.

Components of Campus Ministry

This section examines six specific components of campus ministry—retreats, service, sacraments, prayer, Christian lifestyles, and hospitality—and how they fit in with the entire campus ministry program.

Retreats

Retreats are like a television miniseries. Miniseries are longer than a movie of the week or one sitcom episode. In the same way, retreats are often wider in scope than the other components of a campus ministry program. More adult and student ministers are needed for retreats. Retreats are usually conducted away from the usual environment. If a miniseries is done well, it becomes a one-time special event, which is always remembered for its power, its ability to lift the human spirit, and its inspiration to reflect on the human condition. Think of classic miniseries like *Rich Man, Poor Man* or *Roots*, for example. Good retreats will be recalled for their power, for bringing us into the very presence of God, and for inspiring us to praise and follow our Creator.

Retreats are necessary as a very formative part of any campus ministry program. Retreats allow us to stop and to consider the truly important aspects of life, while at the same time stepping away for a time from the day-to-day responsibilities and work that we must do. Retreats also offer a time for deeper and more informal interaction between faculty, administration, staff, and students. On retreat, we can more easily acknowledge God's presence in our lives and our need for him. Retreats are "mountain-top" experiences that bring us closer to God, experiences that help us to continue in our everyday lives.

There are a number of different retreats that could be part of a campus ministry program, from the faculty retreat, to class retreats, to a core group retreat, to twilight retreats, to special group retreats. This section discusses several different types of retreats.

A *faculty retreat* includes the faculty, the administration, and the staff. All of the people who work in the school have a role to play in the overall atmosphere and ministry of the school. It is wise to include everyone in the retreat and to invite everyone to help with the planning. Although a television show has its stars, all of the people behind the scenes are still credited. The faculty retreat offers a prime opportunity to emphasize the idea that every member of the school staff is a campus minister.

Held early in the school year, a faculty retreat provides a great first step for bonding. However, it can also give a much-needed morale boost if it is held later in the fall or in the middle of the school year. Although the campus ministry director can often lead a very meaningful retreat for the rest of the staff, it can be equally meaningful for the campus ministry director to experience the retreat as part of the staff. There are likely plenty of resources in your diocese from which you can find an outside person to lead the staff retreat.

The most time-consuming retreats in a school setting are the *class retreats*, which usually include an entire class of students, freshmen through seniors. There are many questions to consider in planning class retreats:

✠ *How long will each retreat be (e.g. overnight, two to three nights, or only a few hours)?*

✠ *Will you use a programmed retreat, such as* **Kairos** *or SPIRIT or Reach Out, or will* *you create your own with the help of a team from your school?*

✠ *Which retreats will be off-campus (i.e. might it be better to give the younger classes something to look forward to by holding their retreats on campus and holding the older class retreats off campus)?*

✠ *Will all the retreats be mandatory? If they are mandatory, will you have to schedule more than one for each grade level?*

✠ *Will the campus ministry director lead the retreats or will you ask local youth ministers to lead?*

✠ *Do you have a priest on campus to celebrate the sacraments, or will you have to find a priest from a local parish?*

✚ *How many chaperones will be needed? How will the cost of the retreats be covered?*

✚ *Can the families in your school afford to pay for the costs?*

Offering a retreat for each grade level is important, and the retreat program should build from year to year. Each class will have different needs and these needs will change year by year. Try to take those different needs into consideration. For example, your freshmen might just need a chance to meet their classmates. Sophomores might need to work on cooperation. The juniors may just need to relieve some stress. The seniors may need to be challenged to deepen their relationship with God or define their future goals. Whatever the particular needs of the students at your school, see how retreats can be connected from one year to the next, adding an annual layer to form a cohesive and thematic retreat program.

Many schools also hold retreats for the *student core team* who plan campus ministry events. This might be a group who takes a campus ministry class, elected officers, or a hand-picked group of volunteers. The core group retreat might take place in the late spring or late summer, and it offers an opportunity for the group to bond, to plan, to pray, and to grow in their own relationships with one another and the Lord (see also page 30).

Another possibility for school retreats are *special occasion* or *special group retreats*. Elected student body officers could have their own leadership retreat. Members of an athletic or academic team could have a retreat to build up the group's camaraderie. An evening or afternoon retreat could be offered for any interested students during Lent or Advent. Any of these special occasion or special group retreats may be available on a diocesan level; check the resources in your diocese to see what is offered.

We should also consider the ministry of students who are retreat leaders. Mature juniors and seniors, who possibly have parish experience in ministry, can be very well utilized as retreat leaders for the sophomore and freshmen class retreats. Training for retreat leaders can also often be accessed on the diocesan level. Having student retreat leaders brings positive energy and role models to the retreats as well as developing leadership skills among the students.

Service

....

In some sense, television news programs can be considered the service providers of television. We even attach the title "news service" to their work. Service is an essential part of a Catholic school, and you may find yourself being responsible for many aspects of the student's service work and service learning. This might include a service hour requirement and school-wide service projects (e.g. food or clothing collections, helping families during the holidays, charitable fundraisers, mission collections, etc.) There may also be service clubs on campus. Find out what they do, what projects they organize, and how campus ministry can interact with and support them.

Most Catholic high schools (and some public schools, which may be news to some) have a service component in their plan for student life. It may be a service requirement. If you are responsible for the service component, you have an important job. It can also be a time-consuming job. Hopefully, your school has a working system in place for the service hour program. If not, you may want to research the programs of other schools in your diocese. Find answers to these questions:

✦ *What is a reasonable, yet challenging amount of time to require for service for each grade level?*

✦ *Are students required to donate a certain number of hours to the school and a certain number of hours in their local communities?*

✦ *If students have required hours in a parish confirmation program, can they apply those same hours to the school requirement?*

✦ *How are hours documented?*

✦ *Are service project/organization supervisors contacted in every case or only if there is a question?*

An important aspect of service that is often overlooked is preparation and reflection on the experience. These elements can be grouped under service learning. Preparing students for service might include a volunteer fair, classroom time spent with guest speakers, and aiding students with information and prayer on an attitude of service. Reflection might include class discussion, reflective essays, prayer, and liturgy. Service learning is important because it gives students the opportunity to see their work as a part of ministry and to digest what they have accomplished, to see what they have learned, and to appreciate and recognize God's call in their lives.

Sacraments

Planning and celebrating Eucharist with the student body can be thought of as the "primetime" of high school campus ministry. Eucharist can involve the entire student body, a special group of students, or a particular grade level. It can be celebrated on a special occasion, a holy day of obligation, on retreats, on a daily basis, or in a particular season of the Church year. Whatever the circumstances or the group, the Eucharist lies at the heart of our lives as Catholics.

Some of the practical considerations and questions in this area include:

✦ Is there a priest or pool of priests to ask to celebrate the liturgies?

✦ If you are in a community where few priests are available, is there a deacon or other parish leader who can lead a communion service or prayer service? Is this allowed in your diocese?

✦ Where will you celebrate the liturgy? Is there a chapel on campus, or can you walk to a nearby church? Will all your liturgies be in a school gym or outside on a field?

✦ If you use a gym, how will the seating be set up and arranged?

✦ Who will be your music ministers?

✦ How will you choose readers? How will they be trained?

✠ *Who will take care of setting up and operating any sound system you might need?*

✠ *Who will be your eucharistic ministers? Does your diocese allow students to be eucharistic ministers? If so, how will they be trained?*

✠ *How will the student body be reminded of the need for reverence at the liturgy?*

Planning is a key element in good liturgies. Student input is important, as is drawing upon the experience and creativity of fellow staff members and parents. A liturgy committee composed of members of the aforementioned groups is extremely helpful. If you have a student, staff member, or volunteer who directs music for the liturgy, he or she should be included in planning.

Besides Eucharist, the availability of the sacrament of Penance and reconciliation services for students should be coordinated by campus ministry. Reconciliation can be offered to the school community in a variety of ways. You can offer the sacrament at retreats, especially overnight retreats. It can be offered during the school day on an individual basis with a scheduled class pull-out system, where students sign up ahead of time and then are called out of class to meet the priest in a room on campus. It can be offered to groups of students with a special schedule as a part of a penitential service with individual confession. Again, as with liturgies, the availability of priests will determine the set-up of the availability of the sacrament. Also, as with service activities and required hours, it is important to offer opportunities for students to reflect and examine their consciences prior to confession, and for personal prayer after receiving the sacrament.

Preparation for the sacraments of initiation, or for the sacrament of Confirmation, may be part of your ministry at school, though it is likely done in conjunction with a parish. Unbaptized Catholics may be directed to a parish RCIA process that can be adapted to fit the student's age and school schedule. These sacraments may be catechized through the school's religion classes, as part of your established curriculum. Especially with

Baptism and Eucharist, you may want to establish a procedure to identify students who have not received these sacraments but are interested in receiving them. The procedure may be as simple as asking religion teachers to survey their students, inquiring as to what sacraments they have received, if they are Catholic. This can be followed up with individual contact with any student who has not received a particular sacrament to determine if he or she would now like to prepare for the reception of that sacrament.

Keep in mind the story of Zacchaeus, the tax collector who climbed a tree just to see Jesus but might not have repented if Jesus had not stopped and asked him to come down. Jesus *invited* Zacchaeus to know him and finally said, "The Son of Man has come to search out and save what was lost." There are students we need to invite to meet and know Jesus in the sacraments, and they may be waiting for that invitation. In any case, it would be important to contact a student's parish priest if that student wishes to receive a particular sacrament.

Prayer

The primary component of all our ministry is prayer. Much in the same way that television is always "broadcasting," always offering communication, God is always there, too, offering his constant presence. There are numerous occasions for prayer in a school community, scheduled and unscheduled. You may be responsible in some way for all of these occasions. These might include the opening prayer of each school day, the beginning of each faculty meeting, the opening of parent meetings, the beginning of each class period, the start of athletic contests, and times of special need.

Prayer at the opening of the school day can be very meaningful, but should be short enough to hold the entire student body's attention. This prayer could be traditional, perhaps from the founder of the order that operates the school, and could be the same each day. Perhaps it could also include a scripture passage from the daily readings, or specific readings that reflect on educational needs, or speak to the needs of young people. Special prayers on feast days and during Lent and Advent can bring these days and seasons into focus.

Opening each staff meeting with prayer also helps to keep us focused on the common ministry we share as Catholic educators. Perhaps you could rotate this responsibility among staff members or departments. It would be helpful to offer yourself as a resource person if other staff members are asked to lead prayer at the staff meetings.

Praying at large parent gatherings reminds the school community of our Catholic basis and of the source of our life, who is God. The same can be said of prayer before athletic events, which reminds us that God is the source of our abilities. Prayer can also remind athletes of the need for respect and good sportsmanship.

It would be good to encourage prayer to start smaller parent meetings, athletic practices, student government meetings, and club meetings; again, offer yourself as a resource. Prayer at the beginning of each class in individual classrooms is also extremely important and highlights the role of each staff member as a campus minister. Some teachers may need direction and prayer resources from you.

Special prayer services may be planned for feast days, for the dedication of a building or statue, or for a school anniversary. These special times of prayer, as well as our daily reflection, create an atmosphere that keeps Jesus at our center. Prayer brings us together as a community and fulfills the psalmist's words, "From the rising to the setting of the sun, is the name of the Lord to be praised" (Ps 113:3).

Christian Lifestyles

As television can be educational and even infomercial, campus ministry must promote Catholic vocations and Christian lifestyles. In the past the word "vocations" referred only to religious vocations. Now we can use the phrase "Christian lifestyles," which refers to all of God's callings—to the single, married, and celibate religious life. Probably the most important help campus ministry can offer in this area is an aid in discerning one's vocation. This may also be part of your school's religion curriculum or a specific course. Most dioceses have a vocations office, which works to discover and promote religious vocations. This office may offer the opportunity for discernment groups and probably offers ideas for promoting religious vocations on campus.

If there is a discernment group sponsored by the diocese vocation office, it is probably facilitated by a local sister or priest. Check with local sisters, priests, and brothers to see if any of them would be willing to meet with a group of students who are seeking God's will in their lives. Certainly, there are individuals on your staff who could offer some valuable insight into their own individual experience of God's call.

Hospitality

....

An overriding element that should permeate all of campus ministry and the school community is hospitality. Hospitality is much deeper than providing refreshments of food and drink. We are exhorted in the letter to the Hebrews, "Love your fellow Christians always. Do not neglect to show hospitality, for by that means some have entertained angels without knowing it" (Heb 13:2). One dictionary definition of hospitality is, "treatment, reception, or disposition that is open, generous, cordial, offering a pleasant and sustaining environment." It should be our goal to create a hospitable environment in all aspects of campus ministry. We mainly create hospitality by knowing who people are by name.

The director of campus ministry may not be able to know all about each student, unless the school is very small. So hospitality is the ministry of all staff members. By making sure that all staff members communicate respectfully and confidentially about students' joys and sorrows, achievements and difficulties, and strengths and weaknesses, the staff's knowledge of all the students will blossom. It is the campus minister's task to make sure the staff members are versed in these skills.

As staff members minister to the students, the need for serious healing has the potential to arise. As we know and care for students, they will reveal hurts and problems in their lives. Many times, these problems are beyond the scope of one's professional training and education. In those cases, refer the student to someone who can help. Keep in contact with your administration for advice and for the names of community professionals who can counsel students properly. Refer students with serious needs and problems to those professionals. Be aware of the appropriate agencies within your public school district to which you can refer your students (every public school district must offer services to all students, whether they attend public or private school).

Another possible avenue to encourage hospitality and to facilitate healing may be a peer counseling program. This could be jointly sponsored by campus ministry and a senior leadership class. In any case, it takes planning, training, and care to make it work. Check with other schools in your area to see if they have peer counseling programs and ask for advice if you want to start one. Peer counseling can be very effective and successful if done well and if the students are receptive to it.

Also, a focus group program can help students heal wounds and difficulties. This can be set up through the counseling department and campus ministry too. Here you would have small groups of students with a trained adult facilitator, either from off-campus or from among the staff, where students could focus on a particular issue that they are struggling with in their lives. Issues such as healthy relationships, drug abuse, blended families, and anger management might be topics for these focus groups. Check with your local public school district or county education office to see if it has information or if it provides training for a focus group program.

The Many Details of Campus Ministry

A television show does not come together by chance. There are many people, especially behind the scenes, who perform their specific tasks to cause the final product to emerge. There are also many details in a school setting and campus ministry that have to be taken care of. You are responsible for these details, but it's important that you do your best to delegate. You may not have paid help, but you can rely on volunteers. For some tasks, a student on your campus ministry core team will do a great job. For others, you may need a parent volunteer. Like Jesus' friend Mary, choose the better portion yourself while someone else takes care of the details.

So, what are these details? Let's start with *permission slips*. Whenever you take a group off campus, each youth participant needs a permission slip signed by a parent. This is a must not only for permission to attend the function but also for release of liability and permission for the adult chaperones to seek medical treatment of a minor. These forms should be available at your school. Train your volunteers to check that each student attending an off-campus function takes a permission slip home and brings it back signed.

Another detail is *communication*. This includes fliers, announcements at school, contacting newspapers if you are inviting the public to an event, phone calls to parents about an event, an "office summons" slip to call a student out of class, letters mailed home to parents, reminders to individual students of upcoming events or meetings, information in a parent newsletter, and so on. Communication is obviously an important aspect of any group on campus and can take a lot of time.

Also time-consuming but worthwhile is *keeping track of student schedules*. This is another area where a volunteer can help you. You should keep a list of core group members along with their class schedules and home phone numbers handy. Other lists will be to keep track of students who are scheduled for retreat, working on service projects, or serving as lectors for school liturgies. This information is important, but you don't have to maintain all those lists by yourself.

Fundraising for campus ministry may not be necessary in your school for everyday expenses, but it may certainly be needed for larger events (e.g., retreats) and as a means to collect money for serving those in need. Parents and students alike can be called on to volunteer to help with fundraising, especially in the case of retreats, as a way of cutting the cost per student.

Creating and gathering materials for service activities, retreats, liturgies, and prayer services is an additional detail that can be very time-consuming. Finding some help for the preparation of those activities will help ease your workload.

All of these tasks require delegation skills, organization, planning ahead, and recruiting. Planning ahead is difficult once the school year starts, so use the spring and summer time to plan for next year's activities. Recruiting volunteers may be the most difficult of all. Your campus ministry student core team or campus ministry class will offer a very accessible and enthusiastic group of student volunteers. Realize that the students in your core group are probably members of many clubs on campus and probably volunteer in various capacities off campus.

Request parents of your student core team members to serve as adult volunteers. And make sure campus ministry is listed as one of the volunteer opportunities advertised by the school or parent organization.

Reflection: An Essential Task for Campus Ministers

Television networks take some "time off" each year, during which they show reruns, decide which shows they will keep for the next season, review new shows for consideration, negotiate contracts, etc. In a similar way, we must take time to look back and look forward, to review, to take stock, but especially to pray. In this way we can be sure that our mission and vision are still intact.

This type of reflection can also involve direct self-evaluation and evaluation of our ministry by others. This could take the form of a retreat, activity, or overall program evaluation by students, parents, and/or staff. This can be done informally—in classrooms or staff meetings—or formally with the use of an evaluation sheet.

Reflection should be ongoing with the regular members of your campus ministry team—the students, adults who help at retreats, your administrators, and faculty. In an essential way, reflection is not only done after an event but before as well. Reflection and prayer in preparation for a component of the campus ministry program keep us focused on ministry and that vision we must have.

Jesus certainly gave us an example of reflection in the time he spent in prayer, in the times he went away from the crowd, and in his constant call to everyone to build the reign of God.

Programming
Campus Ministry

Just as television considers the best time for a show and what shows should surround a particular program, campus ministry should consider these items. This requires reflection, calendar planning, and awareness of the students' needs.

There are many events that occur at most high schools, including school-wide fundraisers, homecoming week, student body elections, games, graduation activities, and the like. It is essential to be aware of these big events when planning for campus ministry. The earlier you know your school's master calendar, the better. Start checking in the winter months to find out when these types of events will be scheduled for the following school year. Especially when scheduling senior retreat(s), check the dates for the SAT and ACT to avoid those weekends. Your counseling office should have those dates. Ask your athletic director and coaches for the game schedules for the next school year.

Television also creates an atmosphere, a certain feeling, with its sets or locations on its shows. In campus ministry, we should do the same. If you use a church or chapel for school liturgies, you may want to add a few touches—an altar banner, symbols for a Church season, or other decorations—to the liturgical décor. If your liturgies are regularly held in the gym, it will take more work and preparation to create a good atmosphere for the liturgy. Some planning and consulting with others will result in a less "athletic" environment and one more conducive to worship.

The consideration of place and atmosphere is also important for retreats as well. If you are unfamiliar with retreat facilities in your area, talk to the local parish youth ministers. Visit the retreat facilities to see if they will work for you. Ask these kinds of questions:

✦ *Are there enough beds for the size of your overnight group(s)?*

✦ *Are there meeting facilities large enough?*

✦ *Are there separate dormitories for boys and girls?*

✦ *What else will you need to bring to create an atmosphere that you want?*

Also, for any retreat that is offsite, you will need to check with your school administration to make sure all legal permissions are secured from the parents of students who are participating.

If some of your retreats are on campus, you will certainly need a good indoor meeting space. This might include the gym, a large meeting room, or a chapel. The gym or meeting room may need some work in order to create a proper retreat atmosphere. Banners, posters, balloons, or potted plants might do the trick. If you have good weather and an attractive outdoor area, that would also be a good space to use for a retreat or even for a liturgy, as long as the group is not disturbing any classes that might be in session at the same time.

No matter what, it is always important to consider what your students need and what will motivate or inspire them. Students from different areas may respond differently to different types of music. A retreat or activity that works in a rural area may not work in an urban area.

Campus ministry is definitely a unique opportunity in ministry. Although many of the students you will encounter are in a

Catholic high school by choice, there are those who are not. Many have been "strongly encouraged" by their parents to attend your school. All of them are part of the school community and must be there, at least from eight to three. Usually in parish ministries participation is voluntary. So part of the uniqueness is in the fact that you have a "captive audience." This is true in the classroom as well as on the school grounds, and certainly on mandatory retreats and during mandatory liturgies. In high school campus ministry, we have the opportunity to touch those whom we might not see at a parish youth ministry program.

When I first started in full-time campus ministry, I came directly from a full-time job as a parish youth minister. I thought in some ways that campus ministry would be the same as parish youth ministry. I discovered that it is not.

Part of the difference lies in the "captive audience" situation. Part of it is the group or mob mentality; the same person will act differently in one group or in one situation as opposed to how he or she acts in another group or situation. I have seen students who are quiet and shy at school exhibit loud and outgoing behavior in an outside environment.

A student who is involved in parish youth ministry may be afraid to be seen as "uncool" if he is involved with his high school's campus ministry.

Probably one of the biggest differences I noticed in transitioning from parish youth ministry to campus ministry was the new roles I had to play on campus and in the classroom. While I worked as a youth minister, I did teach a religion class for one year at the local Catholic high school, and it was a disaster. I tried to relate to the students as I did with the young people of the parish. It didn't work. Even when I began my campus ministry position, it took me a few years to learn to develop a workable attitude for myself in the classroom, and to be able to manage the classroom atmosphere.

In my parish youth ministry experience, there was certainly some discipline involved, but the young people always knew me well enough to respond positively and openly to my authority. Being director of campus ministry can be more difficult, especially when you are also teaching. The persona you adopt in the classroom can seem at odds with the persona you have on retreats or in other situations outside the classroom. You may have to be a minister, a counselor, a teacher, a grader, *and* a disciplinarian. It may be difficult for you to be objective in all those roles, and it is probably even more difficult for the students to distinguish among all those roles. You want to be approachable while being able to correct their behavior. You want to show the students you accept them for who they are as individuals while having to evaluate their performance as students. For some individuals, this may be easy; for others, it takes time and experience to find a comfortable combination of the varying roles. Asking Jesus for help and guidance will bring answers; he certainly understands, since he had to play a variety of roles too.

The Role of the Director of Campus Ministry

As director of campus ministry, you are like a television executive in charge of programming. You have a wonderful responsibility and an opportunity to help make a difference in people's lives. You are not alone, however; you will have many good people to help you, advise you, and walk by your side. One of the most important groups to walk with is the group of administrators at your school. Developing a positive working relationship with the principal, vice principal, dean, athletic director, activities director, and any other administrator is essential for the life of campus ministry and for good communication.

Mutual support between the campus ministry director and the principal begins with communication. Your principal may want to approve everything you do, at least generally. Or, he or she may want to just give input on what you are doing, or may give you his or her complete trust. It's always important, no matter which of these situations you find yourself in, to communicate with your principal, keeping him or her informed of your plans, bringing new ideas, asking for input on parents or other adults you are considering asking to help. Your principal will often know things that you might not know but that you *need* to know. If you are not sure ask the question.

Besides all that, it would be important for you to feel that your vision is shared by your principal. Discuss your goals, your philosophy, and the school's mission and charism, so that what you do with that vision is in line with what the principal wants to do, and vice-versa.

You may find that, in your school, you are considered an administrator. Or, perhaps you are at least part of an administrative advisory group or council. This can make your job easier and help you to connect easily with the administration, because you will meet with them regularly. If your position is not considered a part of the administration, you and your principal will need to keep the lines of communication open at all times.

Of course, your communication with the rest of the faculty and staff is also important. Keeping them informed of upcoming events is good public relations, especially when those events affect class or daily schedules. Beyond that, sharing the vision and goals of campus ministry will help the faculty and staff "buy into" the campus ministry program. Sharing the vision will also help the faculty and staff see how they are also campus ministers and will help them assume their individual roles of ministry.

Finally, one of the most important groups to work with is the theology department. It is likely that you will find more adult volunteers for campus ministry among the theology teachers than in any other department. Hopefully, you will also find moral support there. Generally speaking, religion teachers are more willing to take time out of class for campus ministry activities, to communicate campus ministry news to students, and to organize their students for school-wide service projects. Ideally, the goals of the theology department and those of campus ministry are supportive of one another.

A Final Note

Returning to the comparison of campus ministry and television, so much of what is on television is just air, although it is often advertised as reality. We have even referred to what comes to our screens at home as what is on the "air waves." We are well aware, however, that what we see on television is frequently not real, although it surely appears to be.

I definitely think the idea of "air vs. reality" applies to campus ministry. Theories, visions, goals, mission statements, and philosophies inspire us and motivate us, even direct us, but sometimes people think they are just air, not in touch with reality. And I suppose sometimes they are out of touch with reality. They *will* be just air if they are not put into real practice.

What you have read in this chapter and in this book may seem overwhelming or even unattainable, and I would encourage you to be realistic in your expectations in campus ministry, especially if you are just starting out. If you are teaching four or five classes at your school, there is probably only so much you can or should do with campus ministry. Do what you can, given your time limitations. Be realistic about how many activities you can organize, and how often they can occur. Don't try to do everything you have in mind in one year. Give yourself time to get acclimated, to determine needs, to establish relationships and practice hospitality, and to learn. As time goes on, you will develop a volunteer base, a system, and your own style, and you can expand your program without burning out.

If the vision seems too lofty at times and the reality seems too removed from that vision, remember that we are doing God's work, that we are in his service. Remember that we are in the process of building God's kingdom. And remember that when it comes to air and reality, to the vision and the practice, we need them both.

For Reflection

✱ What are ways your campus
ministry program can meet the
needs of your students in the
3 p.m. to 8 p.m. hours?

✱ List some questions you have
regarding the specific
components of campus
ministry—retreats, service,
sacraments, prayer, Christian
lifestyles, and hospitality. Search
out people both on campus and
off campus who can provide you
with answers.

✱ Write a profile of the ideal
student core team member. Also,
write a profile for the ideal
parent volunteer.

✤ *Describe ways you can communicate and collaborate with your principal and administrative staff involving the goals and components of the campus ministry program.*

5

Continuity of the School's Vision and Mission

By Sr. Beatrice Garcia, R.S.M.

St. Paul High School

The task of uncovering the history and culture surrounding a school's original charisms is one that naturally falls under the leadership of the director of campus ministry. Rediscovering and making known these charisms is a way to strengthen campus ministry in any school. It is a way to foster what a school so often advertises—its Catholic identity—in a real and tangible way.

The campus minister can initiate a historical investigation of the founding of the school. Depending on what is discovered, the knowledge can rekindle the spirit of the founding community. This will be a very rewarding experience and a way of celebrating the religious congregations who put much blood, sweat, and tears, as well as priceless resources, into the school's foundation and early years.

If you are blessed enough to have a member of the founding religious community on staff or living nearby, consider video or audio taping the person's remembrances. This piece of history would be a priceless addition to any school's archives. Old yearbooks will give you a place to start with names of religious faculty staff who once worked at the school.

Discovering or rediscovering the foundational richness of your school sets the stage for those given the courage to carry on and keep alive the charism and history of the school. Administration, staff, students, families, alumni, the civic community, and surrounding parishes all influence the life of the school. Tapping the resources of past lay administrators may also provide a wealth of information on the school's traditions and spirit. Staff members with many years of service can add another perspective on the life of the school. Alumni(ae) can add remembrances of the social dimension of student life. In tapping resources, you may also find families with a long history of sending their children to the school. Their perspectives on the changes in the school over the years can be noted and recorded.

If your school is a parish high school, its ties to the parish are obvious. If the school serves surrounding parishes, the nuances of the particular charisms of each parish will demand more intensive research, but the results will make the historical report on school more complete. Another hint: use the diocesan and local community newspaper archives to locate articles and photos that chronicle the history and mission of the school.

Admittedly, this type of research will require much legwork. As director of campus ministry, you should use the same collaborative approach described in other chapters to encourage students, staff, and parents to help you with this work. It is important that the project be initiated by your office, as your ministry will benefit the most from its results.

Gift of Inheritance

The school's charism needs to be cherished as a gift of inheritance. Whether currently strong and visible in the school and in the civic community or a treasure yet to be rediscovered, this reality will strengthen the campus ministry program in any school.

Schools that have newly discovered or have unwittingly carried on these traditions need to insure that they are not taken for granted and risk the chance of them dying and diminishing the Catholic identity of the school.

The charism of the founding community should be shared with all who join the staff community and all students who enroll in the school. All members of the staff invest time and energy into the school and thus should share in carrying on that charism in whatever way they participate in campus ministry. New students—especially the freshman class—should have a program, possibly in connection with a class retreat or through freshman level religion classes, that teaches about the school's foundation, the religious community's founder, the feast day of the patron of the school, history of the school in the surrounding community, and much more.

The upper classes (juniors and seniors) should play a great part in sharing the information on the school's charism with the new students and staff members, thus taking ownership of passing on the history and tradition. They may arrange for a "history week" at the school with various events and liturgies that coincide with this theme. Other appropriate times may be the founder's anniversary of birth or death, the community's special feast day, or other significant times of the year important to the community. As part of the event, the students can be encouraged to develop a logo to be used on posters, pins, and ribbons at a recognition celebration.

Schools close to places where retired sisters, brothers, and priests reside should use the opportunity to invite former faculty and staff members to attend the founding day or event and participate to the extent they are able.

In conjunction with the development office, you might arrange for a joint college scholarship in the name of the religious community to benefit students who have participated in youth ministry. Alumni may be more than willing to participate in this effort, donating funds in the name and memory of a favorite teacher. A scholarship of this kind would assure the memory of the religious community would continue on for many years. This type of effort would surely be much appreciated by the religious community as well.

If your school was not founded or staffed by a religious community and is a parish or diocesan school, the same principles noted above could be utilized to develop founding days or events based on the historical events, important leaders, and patron saints of the parish or diocese.

In whatever form the charisms are shared, the event should be developed with the idea that it will become an annual occurrence at your school directed by you the campus minister.

Perpetuating the Gift

As the principal (and administration) must be versed in other elements of campus ministry so as to offer support, the principal is the vital member of carrying forward and ensuring the life of the school charism. The principal should have a clear understanding of how the charism should be included in the school's philosophy and mission.

The theology department through religion classes can help to perpetuate this goal of making the charism known, lived, and celebrated. An orientation of the school's history and charism should be directed by you at staff and department meetings and retreats. Parents can be encouraged to attend school liturgies and celebrations. You can also include mention of the charism of the school at parent meetings and in newsletters.

The campus minister should consider being designated as the "keeper of the treasure" for the school. This does not mean that you are solely responsible for the work of keeping it a conscious reality in the school, but you are the one who challenges both the faculty and student body to keep the unique spirit alive.

Strong leadership connected with maintaining the charism will make a strong statement to students, staff, alumni, and the neighboring community about the reason for the existence of the school.

Rewards of Being a Campus Minister

The task of a campus minister can seem overwhelming at times. But we must remember that it is not our ministry, it is the ministry of the Lord. Continue striving for balance in your life. Remember that God has only given us this day to live. We must do the best we can in that day. At the end of the day, we need to thank God for blessing us with a chance to minister in all the special ways our job provides. Yes, there will be sad, trying, and exhausting days. There will also be very good, uplifting, and exhilarating days.

You may know times after retreats when it was very obvious that students and staff were touched by the experience.

You may share a time when students come to recount their experience of Christian service as the impetus for continuing service after graduation.

You may be the recipient of a note, a phone call, or a personally given message of appreciation to you from parents about your role in their son's or daughter's lives.

You may enjoy a change in a staff member, from a person reluctant to let his or her students miss class for a retreat, to one of the biggest supporters of campus ministry.

Above all, you may experience those moments when a student who has been struggling to believe in God comes to experience that indescribable love of God that changes his or her life.

What a blessing and a privilege!

For Reflection

....

✝ List at least three things you know about your school's founder(s) and its original charism.

✝ Who is someone who would be a great resource to aid your search into the school's charism?

✝ How can you perpetuate your school's charisms among students, faculty, staff, alumni, and community?

✝ What do you enjoy most about being a campus minister?